Profiles

of

Success

In The
Human Resource
Management Profession

---

by
Gloria W. White, SPHR

College and University Personnel Association

About
CUPA

The College and University Personnel Association (CUPA) is an international network of more than 5,000 personnel administrators representing more than 1,500 colleges and universities. Through regular and special publications and studies, CUPA works to keep its members informed of the latest legal, legislative, and regulatory developments affecting personnel administration, as well as trends and innovative policies and practices in the field. Services include a semimonthly newsletter, a journal, an annual convention, regional meetings, and seminars on timely topics of special interest to the personnel profession. For further information on books of related interest or for a catalog of CUPA publications, contact CUPA at the address below.

Copyright © 1991
by the College and University Personnel Association
Typesetting by Stephanie Hancock
1233 20th Street, N.W., Washington, D.C. 20036
202-429-0311

ISBN: 1-878240-03-X

Table
of
Contents

Foreword v

About the Author vii

Introduction 1

1 Profiles of Success: A Review of the Literature 5

2 The Human Resource Practitioner: A Self-Assessment 15

3 CEOs and the Human Resource Professional 45

4 Internal Clients and the Human Resource Professional 55

5 The External Community and the Human Resource Professional 65

6 Profiles of Success: The 17 Professionals 73

Contributors 89

Bibliography 97

Publications and Research Advisory Board

Foreword

Have you ever wished there was a special formula which would give you the secret to success? Or how about a career strategy that, if followed, would propel you to the top of the ranks in the field of human resource management?

In the absence of such magical formulas, our best bet is to study those who have achieved these goals, learn what it is that makes them successful, and try to build our own abilities in these areas. In this publication, Gloria White has done just that—she has provided us with a highly readable, informal look at the attitudes, traits, and abilities of 17 successful human resource professionals.

This publication does not attempt to be a scholarly survey on the definition of "success," nor should the reader infer that those whose names are not included on these pages are somehow less successful than the 17 professionals profiled here. Rather the reader should find value in deciphering that special combination of characteristics that are common to the literature on the subject, the comments of the individuals profiled, and the statements made by CEOs and colleagues.

For aspiring human resource professionals, this work should

provide much information as they attempt to rise through the ranks. The identification of traits should also help human resource executives and others who are already in leadership positions identify individuals with these talents and then build the right balance of traits into their organizations.

We are indebted to the author for furthering the body of knowledge on success in human resource management and for helping us develop our own formula for success along the way.

> Daniel J. Julius
> Associate Vice President for
> Academic Affairs
> University of San Francisco

About the Author

Gloria W. White is no stranger to success herself, having served the human resource management profession in a variety of leadership roles over the course of her professional career. She currently serves as the Vice Chancellor for Human Resources at Washington University in St. Louis where she is responsible for faculty records, labor relations, AA/EEO functions, benefits administration, personnel, ADA and Title IX implementation.

She received an M.A. in counseling and guidance and a master of juridical studies/law from Washington University and earned her accreditation as a personnel executive from the Society for Human Resource Management. She also holds counseling and teaching certificates from the state of Missouri.

Her involvement with the College and University Personnel Association has spanned two decades and included the key leadership position as President of the Association in 1986 during the development and implementation of the Association's 5-year strategic plan. She has also served as Vice President of Publications and Research (1982-85), chair of the faculty staff relations council, and as a faculty member for various regional and national seminars.

Ms. White has received numerous awards and recognitions for her contributions to the profession. The College and University Personnel Association honored her with the Donald E. Dickason Award—CUPA's highest award for sustained contributions to the human resource profession; the Kathryn G. Hansen Publications Award, for her publication *Personnel Program Appraisal Workbook*; and the Achievement Award for Creativity.

Ms. White currently serves on the Boards of Directors of the CUPA Foundation, the Human Resource Certification Institute, the American Red Cross Bi-State Chapter, the Caring Foundation for Children, Blue Cross Blue Shield of Missouri, and the TIAA-CREF Advisory Board.

Acknowledgements

Expressions of gratitude are frequently exchanged in human interactions for a small deed, a gift, or a kind word. In the case of this project, gratitude is inadequate to convey my appreciation of the contribution of so many to what I believe is a portrait of success in a profession based on understanding the human condition.

I wish to express thanks to the many people who helped to make this monograph possible: to the nominators, the nominees, and referees who so generously provided the material; to Sharon George, my administrative assistant who provided encouragement, assistance, and an always pleasant attitude at the most critical time; to Ed Kelly for his constructive comments on the first draft of the manuscript; to Lourie Reichenberg and Stephanie Hancock of the CUPA publications staff, who produced the final publication; and to Virginia F. Toliver, a cherished colleague and Director of Administration and Planning at the Olin Library of Washington University, who, together with her library colleague Rudolph Clay, Jr., provided extraordinary assistance with the literature search and kept me on track.

Most importantly, I wish to thank my spouse, Glenn, who is always there for me, and who patiently and lovingly interrupted his research to teach me the value and intricacies of word processing. Many thanks to all who gave a golden hand to make this publication possible.

Introduction

The discipline of human resource management has evolved over a period of some 45 years. The profession is rooted in the complexities that human involvement in economic systems which produce goods, provide services, and engage in commerce can bring. The success or failure of each activity depends on people—the human resources—and on the ability of an organization to mobilize those resources to achieve common goals.

People require organizational structure to function effectively. Yet, the people who make up an organization have different skills, training, education, and ideas. These differences require recognition and understanding from enlightened management.

Most organizations are headed by a chief executive officer (CEO) who sets the tone and management philosophy. The value assigned to human resources is determined by that CEO. The CEO's understanding and appreciation of the value of the human resource asset determines whether the human resource function operates on the periphery or in the center of the organization. The chief human resource professional should have the opportunity and responsibility to influence organizational philosophy and the CEO.

This is best accomplished through an understanding of the interrelationship of the organization's parts, backed up by hard data, good judgment, sound and supportable advice, and intimate involvement in setting organizational goals and objectives.

Human resource management theory, philosophy, and practice continue to be expounded by academicians, professionals, associations, and societies as well as by the practitioners through publications, speeches, and in the classroom setting. Yet to be investigated thoroughly are the characteristics of successful human resource professionals as they perceive themselves and as those with whom they interact professionally perceive them.

There is no research that specifically identifies what makes a human resource professional rise up through the ranks of an organization to the top. Our best hope for understanding those who have achieved this status is to try to identify the skills, traits, or characteristics alone, or in combination, that have propelled them to where they are today.

The purpose of this monograph is to determine what, if any, traits effective human resource professionals have in common and then to develop a profile of a successful human resource professional. By identifying and interviewing 17 individuals who were nominated by their peers, their CEOs, and their professional associations as examples of success in the human resource field, we should gain some insight into what makes these individuals tick— what attributes, abilities, and skills have contributed to their success in the human resource field.

Methodology

Information about the human resource professionals profiled here was generated from three primary sources: the nominators, the nominee, and the internal and external colleagues who are referees.

The College and University Personnel Association (CUPA) issued invitations to national associations and acclaimed human resource professionals to submit names and brief supporting statements about individuals who, in the nominators' opinions, were successful.

Nominators were informed that the author would use information from relevant literature and written and oral interviews with nominators and nominees to identify the common characteristics and unique qualities of successful professionals. There was no limit imposed on the number of nominations that could be submitted. In all, 35 human resource professionals were nominated through a nomination form or resume.

Key individuals (i.e., executive directors, presidents, and members) of 10 associations were invited to submit names. The organizations included the American Council on Education, the American Association of Community and Junior Colleges, the Association of Catholic Colleges and Universities, the College and University Personnel Association, the National Association of College and University Business Officers, the National Association of College and University Attorneys, the National Association of State Universities and Land Grant Colleges, the National Association of Independent Colleges and Universities, the Society for Human Resource Management (formerly the American Society for Personnel Administration), and the Washington Higher Education Secretariat.

The second phase of the research included contact with the nominees. Each nominee received written notification of nomination and was asked to respond to five open-ended statements. In addition, each nominee was asked to list the names, titles, addresses, and telephone numbers of five individuals who had in-depth knowledge of his or her professional performance.

Fifty-one percent of the nominees responded to the questionnaire. Four nominees (11 percent) responded but declined to participate due to company policy or for personal reasons. The remaining 38 percent did not respond.

The third and final collection of information came from the CEOs, peers, scholars, and subordinates who were familiar with the nominee's performance as a human resource professional. These sources provided relevant data to develop a profile of the characteristics common to successful human resource professionals.

1

Profiles of Success: A Review of the Literature

"A professional is one who does the right thing because doing the right thing is the right thing to do—whether or not anyone is monitoring." [1]

Success as a human resource professional depends on several factors. Destanick wrote that:

"If you understand your profession—and your company's business and goals—you are halfway up the road to success. The rest of the formula requires positioning yourself in your company's senior management. And this can only be done by defining your role—to yourself and your organization." [2]

Put another way, Destanick identified four elements of a successful human resource function which he defines as the "acid test for measuring effectiveness." The four elements are:

1. Understanding the business,

2. Addressing strategic business needs,
3. Positioning the human resource function as a senior management discipline, and
4. Developing good consulting and marketing skills. [3]

The human resource professional plays a growing role in the overall success of the organization as underscored by a recent *Wall Street Journal* article which identified several factors as the impetus for moving human resource managers from the passive administrators of the 1980s, to the proactive managers of the 1990s. These factors include the changing demographics of the workforce and the corporate perception of personnel professionals as strategic managers of a major asset—the human being.

This new mode of thinking thrusts the human resource professional into the limelight of visibility and accountability. Solomon stresses that this new visibility requires the right "fit" between the human resource professional and the chief executive officer since the value assigned to human resources is determined by the CEO. Job security for the human resource professional, especially in higher education, may depend not only on the right fit between the two individuals, but on the CEO's tenure, as well.

Essentials of Success
The following three abilities are identified by Fitz-enz as essential to measuring success in the human resource function:

1. The ability to do your job.
2. Excelling in the right areas.
3. Measuring your performance and using the results to obtain the resources you need.[4]

Fitz-enz discusses the various audiences that the human resource function serves and the model of efficiency and productivity, all of which contribute to establishing the human resource professional as a key member of the management team.

Predicting Leadership Behavior

While the foregoing literature focuses on the characteristics necessary to achieve success as a human resource professional, studies also have been conducted in the last 10-15 years to identify variables that measure career success and leadership qualities in general.

Psychologists and other behaviorists have researched what particular human qualities contribute to the achievement of success. One component of success—leadership skill—was the subject of several studies, including two that specifically addressed personality traits of leaders as predictors of leadership behavior A later study conducted by Atwater set out to identify the importance of situational and individual variables in predicting leadership behavior. Her hypothesis is the antithesis of the two earlier studies.[5]

Bass and Dunteman found personal orientation (self, task, or interaction orientation) to be associated with patterns of leadership.[6] Another study by Fleishman and Salter demonstrated that individuals with more empathic personalities tended to display more considerate leadership behavior.[7] Both studies concluded that personality traits were the antecedent of leadership behavior.

Interpersonal Skills are Key

Atwater's research suggests that factors other than personality traits trigger leader behavior. She cites interpersonal trust and subordinate loyalty in an organization as being important to creating a successful leadership climate:

"Factors most predictive of supportive supervisory behavior (e.g., resolving conflicts, supporting opportunities for improvement for workers, inspiring loyalty) were the levels of trust and loyalty expressed by subordinates toward their supervisors. The more trust and loyalty expressed the more positively the supervisor was perceived to behave."[8]

The significance of interpersonal relations to success was confirmed in other studies. In 1969, Glickman concluded that skill in interpersonal relationships is the key to success in management.

"Skill as a leader and in relating to others is a most important requirement at all levels of management. At the top of the corporation the group of consequence is relatively small. Its members have highly personal relationships. They interact with one another as in a small firm. A high proportion of group involvement is usual. Informal procedures supplant formal ones."[9]

Leaders vs. Managers

While interpersonal skills appear to be instrumental to success in management, they are certainly not the only factors involved. For example, Andrews conducted research in which he pinpointed the difference between leadership and supervision. He said, "Leaders manage and managers lead but the two are not the same."[10]

The outstanding leader who initiates, takes risks, and finds new paths to travel may even run afoul of the interpersonal relationship factor. The Andrews study concluded that the creative style of the outstanding leader "may conflict with the demands for reliability and conformance to organizational rules and constraints displayed by the effective administrator."[11]

Other Traits Identified

Other studies linked career success with self perception, gender, career mobility, career planning, and career satisfaction.[12]

Korman, Wittig-Berman, and Lang found that self-perception often conflicts with other people's views. Successful managers often were not satisfied with their careers and did not feel successful or proud of themselves. They had their own internal perspectives of success, which would often lead them to subjectively consider themselves failures.[13]

A study of careers conducted by Gattiker and Larwood linked success to the importance of the position in an organization and whether the position permits access and use of power.[14] The study cited Locke's caution about career planning or strategies. Locke warned that reliance on career planning strategies as keys to success and job satisfaction will cause strategists to credit career success to strategy rather than performance. He went on to conclude that career strategy may not always explain objective career success.[15]

Gattiker concludes that the literature is biased towards examining the relationship between objective predictors such as social demographics and income, and that researchers ignore relationships between subjective predictors such as career strategies, perception of career success, and career satisfaction.

A Note on Women and Minorities

The literature on career success normally addresses predictors of success among the general population. However, there have been three significant studies of career success specifically among women.

The Gattiker study mentioned earlier found that gender affects career achievement and that women attained higher management positions at a later career stage than men.

Wilkins and McCullers studied 80 women in the fields of medicine and law in atypical and traditional careers. Their research found that women who achieved success in atypical careers had experienced play patterns similar to males as children. There was strong family support for achievement and the family unit was usually intact. The women in the study had not been required to do household chores as children. Their mothers were perceived as positive influences and sources of emotional support. In contrast, Wilkins and McCullers called attention to the opposite view of mothers presented in prior literature, which paints the mothers of achieving women as rather hostile, critical, and rejecting.[16]

Romero and Garza studied attributes for success or failure among Anglo, Black, and Chicano women. Minority women showed a greater tendency to attribute employment successes and failures to the individual's race and national origin. In contrast Anglo women were more likely to attribute success or failure to other factors. Romero concluded that Anglo women appear to be "color blind."[17]

Offermann compared the genders in a study of the visibility and evaluation of male and female leaders. The results of Offermann's research showed that females who lead mixed sex groups are predicted to have greater future success than females who lead all male or all female groups.

A subsequent study by Offermann suggests that sex stereotyping may no longer be a major factor in assessing leadership qualities in females. Females who were observed outside a laboratory environment (i.e., in a field setting with a range of options) responded in ways similar to males.[18]

Conclusion

This brief literature review reveals a number of recurring factors as predictors of potential career success. Research has identified myriad personality traits and professional skills that are correlated with success in leadership and management behavior. Destanick mentions understanding the business and positioning the human resource function. Fitz-enz stresses excelling in the right areas. Atwater cites trust and loyalty; Fleishman and Salter stress empathy; Glickman concludes that skill in interpersonal relationships is the key to success.

Combining the traits and characteristics that are identified in the literature results in the following list of 17 traits and skills that are correlated with career success:

* ability to do the job
* excelling in the right areas
* using good judgment
* understanding the profession
* understanding the organization's goals
* positioning the human resource function in senior management
* developing good consulting and marketing skills
* being a strategic manager
* working well with the CEO
* using power appropriately
* possessing good leadership skills
* developing trust and loyalty of subordinates
* good interpersonal relationships
* being a risk taker
* creativity
* visibility and accountability
* compatability of personality traits

It is possible to combine these skills, traits, and characteristics into five broad categories:

1. technical proficiency
2. proactive orientation
3. communication skills
4. integrity
5. flexibility and adaptability

Each category is further defined below.

1. *Technical Proficiency*— the ability to do the job effectively.

Understanding the profession, the organization, and its goals. For human resource managers, this would include an in-depth understanding of laws and regulations affecting the human resource function as well as the organization's mission.

2. *Proactive Orientation*—the ability to "make things happen." This includes strategic planning and positioning the HR function as part of the senior management team. Proactive orientation also includes excelling in the right areas and motivating others to excel. A proactive manager is the opposite of a reactive manager—one who acts to make events happen, rather than reacts to what has already occurred.

3. *Communication Skills*—the umbrella term for skills that are necessary to develop and maintain good interpersonal relationships. Communication skills include management and leadership skills, empathy, compatability of personality traits, and working well with people at all levels from the CEO to subordinates.

4. *Integrity*—"doing the right thing." Trust, loyalty, good judgment, visibility, accountability, and using power appropriately are all a part of integrity.

5. *Flexibility and Adaptability*—the ability to see "the big picture," to identify and prepare for long-term trends; creativity and risk-taking.

These five categories, as drawn from the literature, provide some insight into the characteristics common to successful human resource professionals. But will these five traits synchronize with the comments of the CEOs? Are they the same traits identified by the individuals profiled in Chapter Two? Are they also the traits that internal and external clients see as important?

Notes

1. Yoder & Heneman, ASPA Handbook.
2. Destanick, "What Makes HR Successful?," 41.
3. *Ibid.*
4. Fitz-enz, J. "HR Measurement," 53.
5. Atwater, "Relative Importance," 290.
6. *Ibid.*
7. *Ibid.*
8. *Ibid.*
9. Andrews, "Leadership and Supervision."
10. *Ibid.*
11. *Ibid.*
12. See also: Batlis & Green, "Leadership Style Emphasis," 587; Gattiker & Larwood, "Career Success," 75; and Steinberg, "Climbing the Ladder of Success."
13. Korman, et al., "Career Success," 342.
14. Gattiker & Larwood, "Predictors for Managers' Career Mobility," 569.
15. *Ibid.*
16. Wilkins & McCullers, "Personal Factors," 343.
17. Romero & Garza, "Attributions for Occupational Success," 14.
18. Offermann, "Visibility and Evaluation," 533.

2

The Human Resource Practitioner: A Self-Assessment

The next step in identifying successful human resource traits is to compare the five traits we pulled from the literature with the perceptions of the 17 human resource practitioners selected.

Each practitioner was asked to respond to open-ended statements that were phrased to elicit their perceptions of themselves as well as to provide objective assessments of qualities that they believe are essential to achieving success. The open-ended statements used to generate these responses were:

1. "It is probable that I was nominated for inclusion in this study because . . ."
2. "As I look back on the many aspects of my involvement in the human resource profession I have gained the greatest satisfaction from . . ."
3. "If I stop to review my personal and professional life, the things that I would do the same and the reasons are. . ."
4. "The things that I would do differently and the reasons are . . ."
5. "The qualities that I believe to be essential to living a full and productive life are . . ."

The Practitioners Speak

In order to focus the attention of the reader on the specific characteristics rather than on the individual person, the 17 individuals nominated by their peers will not be identified by their correct names. Biographical sketches of these professionals will appear later.

Many of the traits mentioned here fit into one of the five categories we identified from the literature.

Andy Adams

Andy Adams believes he was nominated for inclusion in this study because of his visibility as an adjunct MBA program faculty member of a major research university, his role as former president of an international human resource professional association, and his current position as chief human resource officer for a Fortune 100 company.

He states that his greatest satisfaction has been derived from playing a significant role in the emergence of his company. He also gains professional satisfaction from implementing policies, developing the professionalism of personnel, teaching, writing, and national speaking engagements.

In his words, the qualities essential to living a full and productive personal and professional life are:

* Having a good work ethic and nurturing it.
* Respecting the value systems of others.
* Trying to grow in some way, every day.
* Maintaining good health.
* Learning effective use of time.
* Surrounding himself with good people.
* Being selfless in judgments.
* Recognizing the importance of balancing family, business, and recreation.

Pat Able

Pat Able achieved her success in the profession through a non-traditional career path. She said she arrived at this stage by taking risks, being mobile, and gaining on-the-job experience. She candidly assessed her career path.

She was a product of the '50s, she said, at a time when "women were expected to be satisfied with marriage and having babies. Working outside the home was a necessity to move the family forward." However, at some point, her job became a career which she actively sought to advance.

"I enrolled in as many evening classes as responsibilities would permit. I took advantage of training opportunities and I never turned down the offer or assignment of additional duties. This mind set has provided a considerably diverse background.

By 1983, I had reached a prized position in county government. Only one problem existed—the marriage was coming to an end. Considering myself in tune with the '80s, I decided it was time to experience living alone. So, after 30 years of marriage and 47 years of living, I divorced, changed my name, quit my position with the county government, turned my home over to my eldest daughter, and returned to the west to start over again.

Today I am further challenged in the 'people business' with a trend I perceive for the '90s—Empowering people to make decisions in a flatter organization. Human resource management remains an on-going and stimulating profession."

What does Able believe are essential for a full personal and professional life?

* Being open to people and ideas;

* Having a sense of humor;
* Enjoying both men and women for their differences and sameness;
* Maintaining an eternal optimism by keeping the glass half full; and
* Looking for ways to give back. She strongly believes civic and community participation is a necessary part of rounding out a productive life.

Tom Jones

Tom Jones has moved rapidly up the human resource career ladder. He suggested that the visibility of the human resource function he heads probably contributed to his nomination for this study. "The human resource division of my institution is looked upon, both internally and externally, as a seasoned and capable unit." Jones stressed the importance of visibility, excellence, and credibility in his management philosophy and professional objectives.

"My personal contributions to the field of human resources have been fairly visible, including national, regional, and local contributions to professional associations, teaching, and professional consulting. I have always attempted to instill among the professional staff the importance of 'contributing back' to the profession, whether such contributions be in the form of teaching, research, or professional service. Contributing back and staying current is critical to whatever success I have enjoyed."

He also pushes people to achieve their top potential.

"Challenging employees to fulfill their own capacity and abilities has been rewarding. While one can always point to outside constraints that prevent accomplishing objectives, my advice to the staff has always been that 90 percent of the time the biggest roadblock to accomplishing objectives is themselves."

Jones does not think he could have chosen a field of endeavor more suitable to his own personal make-up than human resource management.

"It is a blend of the more empirical side of management (statistics, research, finance/benefits, actuarial projections, and compensation management) and the more subjective aspects of management (labor relations, human resource development, psychology, and sociology) which together have a critical impact on the institutional or corporate culture of an organization. As a practitioner, creating innovative compensation practices, being responsible for corporate labor relations, and being a part of the overall executive management team, has been professionally satisfying."

Jones focused on sensitivity, empathy, and loyalty as essential qualities for a full life and also mentioned such traits as: "caring, optimism, goal-directed, results-oriented, integrity, hard-working, creative, persevering and demanding."

"Probably the most important, though, is having the sensitivity and capacity to place yourself in the shoes of another, which allows for understanding of a person's motivation, whether it is a member of the family, colleague, CEO, or subordinate."

He also mentioned the following traits as being important to personal and professional success:

* Taking life seriously, but also finding humor.
* Maintaining a balance between family and work.
* Reinforcing a person's positive strengths, rather than dwelling on weaknesses.
* Being loyal to superiors and subordinates.

Karen Baker

Karen Baker said she gains satisfaction from "being part of a challenging and demanding profession which requires continual updating of specialized knowledge."

"I have often heard human resource professionals remark that many of the situations they handle would provide interesting copy for a book. Indeed, much of my satisfaction comes from the challenge of working with a diverse number of employee relations situations, all of which prove to be unique as well as unpredictable."

Baker divides the essentials for a full, productive personal and professional life into "saintly virtues and mortal realities."

"If I were to make a list of the personal characteristics which hiring supervisors most frequently mention in describing their ideal candidates, I could use such a list to describe the attributes of those human resource managers who are leading the fullest and most productive personal and professional lives. On such a list are all the saintly virtues, such as integrity, honesty, tolerance, compassion, loyalty, and dedication.

In addition to striving for high marks on all the saintly virtues, I believe successful human resource professionals must have a high tolerance for ambiguity and a talent for managing multiple and shifting priorities. Because our responsibilities are impacted by individual and organizational behaviors, we find that new and unexpected situations arise each day and that each case brings with it a unique set of circumstances and challenges. Even those employee relations matters which start out to be seemingly routine and repetitive inevitably end up having unexpected and unpredictable twists to them.

A positive consequence of choosing a career which involves selecting and evaluating others on these traits is that human resource professionals can, it is hoped, more readily recognize when there is a need to improve their own ratings."

Richard Brown

Richard Brown is a leading human resource professional in a multi-college community college district. He believes this background has contributed to his success.

"It has been my very good fortune to have been employed for the past 30 years in large community college systems which have been innovative, forward looking, and willing to take risks. The CEOs for whom I have worked have encouraged me to become involved with and to take on the issues.

For example, while in California, I had the opportunity to participate (on a statewide basis) in decision making regarding how to manage the effects of mandatory public sector collective bargaining. Tax reform issues also allowed me to get involved in major restructuring tasks as higher education faced new financial challenges."

Brown says his current employer has continued and even amplified, this encouragement toward innovation.

"I have been encouraged to support the development of human resource programs which are responsive to employee needs and which are innovative and unique. These programs, in every case, have been employee driven. I have been given the freedom to provide an environment which permits the kind of risk taking that results in successful programs.

Because of our size and visibility the innovative programs (e.g., flexible benefits, internships, apprenticeships, wellness programs, managed care, point-of-service medical programs, EAPs, faculty hiring pools, recruitment activities) have been given much favorable nationwide exposure and recognition."

From Brown's perspective, integrity, compromise, and caring pave the road for a full and productive life. He asserts:

"My success or lack thereof has been determined, in great measure, by whether or not I am perceived as being totally and completely honest. I learned early in my career that people want an honest and straightforward answer."

As far as compromise, he advises,

"Accept the fact that most successful endeavors come about as a result of compromise. It is difficult for some to realize a compromise is nothing more than creating an environment in which all parties can be winners. When everyone wins, goals are attained much more quickly and with much less stress. It is not at all contradictory to believe that one can have integrity and still have the ability and willingness to compromise."

Caring, he says, is learning to understand.

"It has become more important to me to understand and recognize individual differences, needs, desires, and wants. It took me far too long to recognize that everyone did not grow up with the same set of experiences and background. A quality that I wish I personally had in greater quantity than I do is the ability to accept each and every individual at face value and to attempt not only to understand, but appreciate that individual."

Jack Smith

Jack Smith is credited with managing dramatic change in the state-of-the-art human resource function that is in operation at his agency. He attributes his success to his flexibility, management skills, and ability to face challenges head-on.

"This agency has changed dramatically since I became director, and my staff members are cognizant of this fact. We now recognize that the achievements of an organization come from the combined efforts of each individual working toward common objectives. Staff members have assisted in clarifying the purpose of their positions through development of vision statements, written policies, and procedures. Individual staff members are not only well aware of the expectations placed on them but have helped to determine those expectations."

He summed up his management philosophy with the following statement:

"I expect and receive from my staff their best efforts. I am always willing to hear and consider suggestions. Intelligence, creativity, quality work, and enthusiasm are recognized and rewarded by promotion and employee recognition programs. I am a strong proponent of the team concept and strive to have everyone realize what an important part of the organization they truly are."

Smith describes the qualities essential to achieving a full and productive professional and personal life as:

* Knowing what you want to achieve professionally and personally and working to obtain those goals.
* Being able to recognize, nurture, and make use of your talents.
* Using your intelligence and receiving the education needed to use that intelligence.
* Quality verbal skills which will enable you to develop rewarding and fruitful relationships.
* Respecting others so they respect you.
* Being sensitive, understanding, and responsive to the needs of those around you.
* Having and projecting a positive attitude.
* Being motivated and motivating others.
* Being conscientious and efficient.
* Surrounding yourself with people who can accomplish what is needed and then empowering them with the opportunity and resources to succeed.
* Being able to prioritize and to balance family, social relationships, and career responsibilities.

Ben Cook
Ben Cook is a successful human resource consultant to

government and higher education. In his personal assessment of his success he cited the extensiveness of his experience.

"I have spent virtually all of my professional life serving in a variety of human resource positions in higher education institutions across the nation. I began my career at the inception of public sector and higher education faculty collective bargaining and have acted as a consultant to governments and colleges and universities to assist them in accommodating this new phenomenon. I have written extensively in this area."

Cook says his greatest satisfaction is derived from "developing new and innovative ways to solve problems. Human resource professionals are dealing with constantly fluctuating problems as society's values change and institutional goals respond. The new problems posed by the superimposition of collective bargaining on the traditional personnel processes call for creative responses. This has been the most interesting aspect of this field."

He said his recipe for a good life and professional fulfillment would include these ingredients:

* Good health first and foremost.
* A good partner with whom to share life and to help in escaping daily stress.
* Talented colleagues with whom to interact.
* A challenging set of problems.
* A sense of humor to help in coping.
* Physical activity to offer a respite from the mental aspects of a career, and,
* Opera (to add the "sublime to the daily drudgery").

Betty White

Betty White is a philosopher who is nationally recognized as an expert in employee benefits. She attributes her nomination to this recognition.

"In the past 10 years I have presented 40 papers and conducted many seminars for higher education professionals in human resources, business and finance, and academic administration. The last decade has presented the higher education community with unprecedented challenges. My work in professional development has assisted the higher education community address those challenges."

She says these accomplishments have helped her current institution as well.

"Each topic I've addressed, each seminar I've presented, each problem I've studied was related to a program challenge that we wanted to address organizationally. Being asked to present the topics to external audiences has allowed me to share my efforts and to ensure that the organization benefits from the extensive study and analysis required for national presentations."

White offers seven qualities she considers essential to satisfaction in life:

1. Developing a commitment to life-long learning. Not limiting your interests to just human resources or defining your position by an organizational chart.

2. Spending your life overall as a generalist and each year as a technical specialist—in whatever is being

demanded of you by your organization, by yourself, or by Congress.

3. Working hard and caring deeply about your friends, your family, your hobby, and whatever else you love.

4. Rejecting complacency.

5. Valuing the needs, opinions, and wishes of others. Respecting opposing views.

6. Accepting the legislative changes we are presented with in human resources as ultimately being positive forces. Looking past the extra work and accepting the fact that employment and benefits legislation have created a better society.

7. Valuing the dignity of each person.

Ted Thomas

Ted Thomas says he tries to balance his roles of company conscience and employee advocate and believes that his success in doing so earned him the nomination for this study.

"The human resource function in my company, during my leadership, has become a major partner in the management of the company. Our plans, programs, and implementation efforts are closely tied to the strategic plan. As a result, our efforts in such areas as management development and education, manpower planning, equal employment opportunity, compensation and benefits, labor relations, employee relations, and health and safety, are well thought of and effective both internally and externally."

He says his professional activities have also played a role in how his peers see him.

> "I have been active in various human resource organizations and have chaired the Employee Relations Committee of the Business Roundtable, and currently chair the Labor Policy Association. I have been an industry spokesman on various legislative matters in Washington, D.C. and was appointed by former Labor Secretary Elizabeth Dole to the National Commission of Achieving Necessary Skills. It would indicate that I am well respected by my peers. We also have the best of labor relations with our unions and I believe I am well respected by the union leaders."

For Thomas, the qualities necessary to have a full and productive professional and personal life are:

* Getting a good education—including writing, communications, and problem-solving skills.
* Striking a balance between business and personal life, recognizing, however, that success requires hard work and long hours.
* Having compassion for people.
* Developing some interests outside of work, and
* Giving something back to society and the community.

Al French

Al French has broad experience as a human resource professional for both the profit and not-for-profit sectors. Like some of the other nominees, he ties his success to professional activities.

> "I'm a joiner who finds informal networking and social activity useful. Such activity produces a level of visibility

and range of relationships that result in recognition. I believe in freely sharing experiences and in continuous efforts to learn from the experiences of others."

He believes his longevity in the human resource area may have played a part in his nomination. He also believes his experience and exposure to some of the top human resource issues have contributed. He said,

"Another factor might include being part of the moral revolution in regard to plans for progress, equal opportunity, affirmative action, diversity, and multi-culturalism in the workplace. The personal, professional, and organizational struggle to achieve an environment of universal respect have generated the most challenging and satisfying experience for me in personnel administration."

According to French, being involved and nurturing relationships are essential for personal and professional fulfillment. In his words:

"Balancing the time and energy invested in personal activity provides the basis for a life grounded on physical, emotional, and spiritual health. Personal relationships provide the support necessary to achieve fullness and productivity. Giving and accepting support, respect, help, care, and love sum it up for me."

Paula James

Paula James, a practitioner in a medical environment, characterizes herself as an influential leader and a concerned listener who transfers her beliefs to her work. She believes her dedication to the human resources field landed her the nomination for this study.

"It is probable that I was nominated for inclusion in this profile because of the evidence of my dedication to the human resource field as a profession and the respect and support my current institution gives to the role of human resources. I believe in our profession. We are a combination of counselor, social worker, activity director, business manager, and internal consultant—the list is endless. I have had the opportunity to work at four very diverse organizations in the past 20 years and was able to leave the first three feeling that I had made some contributions to positive change. This has enabled me to maintain an excellent network of people in various professions."

This opportunity extends to her current job, which she says has brought out some new talents.

"My employer encourages creativity and I have found a talent for this which was formerly unrealized. Few organizations have initiated as many employee programs as this one has in a five-year period. Although these have not all been easy or popular at first, over time our 'team' worked to educate and visibly show a concern and support to the employees. This is recognized in our county where we are considered to be the 'best place to work.' "

Her essentials for professional and personal fulfillment include:

* Developing a sense of synergy—the ability to bring information and people from various, often unrelated sources and places, to a common understanding.
* Maintaining a sense of balance in personal and professional life.

* Being actively involved. Joining an organization and becoming involved in a leadership or committee role.
* Believing in others—family, professional acquaintances, community. Developing a desire to assure that people and groups thrive.
* Possessing insight. Going beyond the simple, most obvious answer and considering many alternatives. Being creative; developing problem-solving skills.
* Having standards. Everyone needs a foundation. This can be a religion, a set of ethical principles, or a set of beliefs.
* Keeping a positive, optimistic outlook on life.
* Fostering a love of learning and continual education.
* Persevering. Developing the attitude that "this too shall pass" during difficult times and being able to enjoy the good times.

Jackie Big

Jackie Big was described by her nominator as the ideal human resource professional because she "knows the substance, content, and issues of the field." Jackie attributes this image of success to several factors:

"I have served as a leader in the human resource profession not only in my employment arena but also within the broader arena of human resource management. I have used my role in these communities to further enhance the profession.

I have assumed an active role in my professional association by conducting research, writing, and speaking on emerging issues in the profession. I have also served the profession by teaching extensively and serving as a consultant."

She says she has applied these skills to her daily management tasks.

"I have created a human resource program in my organization that emphasizes organizational effectiveness through maximizing the human potential. The personnel systems I created serve to strengthen the culture which was established for this purpose. I am frequently called upon by chief executive officers to develop policies, lead staff development programs, and serve as an organizational consultant."

Big says her greatest satisfaction is serving as a change agent in the development of new organizational cultures for her employer.

"From a climate lukewarm to any suggestion for change, I built an affirmative action program. I take pride in moving my employment environment from its white male dominated environment to one where women may achieve equally with men, not only in terms of their roles but also in their paychecks.

We have moved from an organization of individual fiefdoms to one with pervasive synergy. All jobs are deemed important; excellence is required of everyone. We have developed a strong performance appraisal program that supports this premise and that really works."

Her philosophies about life's essentials include:

* If you do what you love, success will follow. Individual growth can only come about by a willingness to take an inner journey, to examine your life, and to value introspection. In turn, one must be willing to work on the "warts."

* Spiritual grounding, she says, has been an important part of her personal and business success and has been responsible for her high energy and commitment.
* Maintain a balanced life with time for developing the physical, intellectual, spiritual, and social dimensions.

Jane Doe

Jane Doe describes herself as proactive and persuasive, characteristics she believes resulted in her nomination as an example of professional success.

"I have an excellent reputation in the broad field of human resource management at the national, regional, state-wide, and campus levels. I am highly creative, yet practical, and have an ability to design state-of-the-art programs, models, and paradigms. I have strong visionary and leadership skills and the ability to take risks. I have a breadth of involvement in voluntary and civic activities, most of which are directly relevant to human resource management. I am an excellent teacher at the graduate level as well as at the consultant, supervisory, and training levels."

She says these experiences have brought her diversity. "I have a breadth of knowledge across many disciplines relevant to human resource management." As a result, she has "an ability to work and envision at both the micro-levels and macro-levels of practice and policy."

The principles that Doe says she ascribes to for professional and personal fulfillment are:

* A strong code of ethics.
* Having a sincere, deep concern for people—their worth, and their dignity—at work and with friends and family.

* Living what you believe.
* Having a high value for education and not being afraid to be in a constant state of learning.
* Having high standards for excellence and developing the leadership skills to show individuals and groups these higher visions.
* Having resilience to survive criticism—learning from the critics and incorporating what has merit and not being influenced by non-meritorious ideas.
* Being creative both at work and in your personal life.
* Developing the ability to examine issues from many frames of reference.
* Being able to empathize and remain objective.

Jim Davis

Jim Davis is able to joke about his successful career which has spanned four decades in human resources. When asked to state what characteristics he possesses that others might view as indicative of success in the profession, he quipped: "Either, someone was trying to overcome a latent prejudice against Italians, or someone likes short people!"

On a more serious note, he attributes his image as a success to his many years in the industry.

"I became a higher education personnel professional in 1948. At that time very few employers had personnel departments. I have published a great deal in the higher education personnel field and have made many presentations at meetings. I have always tried to get to know as many fellow professionals as possible to pick their brains for things they are doing well so that I could improve my programs."

Davis said this long career, followed by a "retirement" that has included consulting for 30 institutions, has provided him plenty of time to ponder what has made his life so satisfying. He said it includes:

* Developing young staff members. "Over my 38 years I hired a lot of beginners in personnel work. It was my pleasure to see five of them end up heading human resource offices at major institutions. All five had started on my staff with no personnel experience. What greater legacy and joy could there be?"

* Getting things done through others. "I learned to trust others as long as they are informed. I believe in training, trusting, and post-auditing rather than handling everything from central administration."

* Being responsible for faculty as well as staff personnel administration. "While handling the faculty personnel administration differs in style from handling other staff affairs, having some responsibility for both sides of the house provides the opportunity to do a better total job. I was fortunate to have responsibilities in both areas."

* Having my word trusted. "I worked very hard to have people at all levels understand that when I gave information or made a commitment, my word could be trusted. For example, although the teamster officers and I disagreed on some issues, they were kind enough to tell me that if I told them something, they knew that it was an honest presentation of the facts. Integrity is particularly important for personnel professionals."

* Planning. "I worked very hard at anticipating needs rather than reacting to problems. Having plans made in advance for contingencies is important, but equally important is having the president and other key policy makers alerted in advance so that those plans are accepted."

* Productivity and minimized costs. "As the key person making personnel policy recommendations, I tried to be aware at all times of the need for those policies not to inhibit productivity or create unusual and unforeseen costs."

* "Most important, though, is to have a sense of humor, no matter what happens; it really helps."

Pam English

As with other nominees, Pam English points to her active involvement in a number of human resource management professional associations on local, regional, and national levels as contributing to her success. She said that involvement has given her "the opportunity to interact professionally with a diverse group of human resource management practitioners representing a variety of companies and institutions throughout the United States. More importantly, it has given me the opportunity to develop lasting personal and professional friendships with a group of colleagues who are unfailing in their willingness to share information and ideas."

English says her greatest satisfaction comes from working hard at solving complex organizational dilemmas and being part of the group which eventually creates 'elegant administrative solutions.'

"The satisfaction of being part of hard-working, creative

groups has come from many sources. These include special project work with administrative and faculty colleagues throughout the institutional system of campuses, service on local and state-wide policy advisory committees, work with higher education colleagues from throughout the United States on consulting jobs, elected service on national and regional boards, and most certainly, the daily work with the staff of the System Personnel Division."

Her work has often led her to her state capital.

"I have also experienced great satisfaction by being in a position to influence legislative or regulatory matters pertaining to human resource management in the state. Although success in this area is by no means assured on any given issue, the process is fascinating regardless of the outcome."

English's formula for personal and professional success would include:

* Having a well-developed and frequently used sense of humor and having a spouse with at least the same, if not better, sense of humor.
* Since there is no lack of ego in the upper levels of higher education administration, self-confidence, not to be confused with self-importance, is required.
* Having the knowledge to do a job and commiting the time and energy to stay current on the issues.
* Flexibility, as long as it does not deteriorate into laxity and inconsistency.
* Having a thick skin and not taking either the bad or the good times too personally.

* Having fun in both the personal and professional aspects of life.

Jerry Ames

Jerry Ames credits his success to professional experience in six different organizations which has provided him an ability to analyze issues, provide advice, and make decisions.

"During my career in human resources spanning 26 years, I have remained challenged and active in the field. I have written syllabi for seminars on human resources, and I have taught numerous seminars. Much of the writing required research or review of related literature which provided me with more knowledge about human resources. I have benefited in my career from having had the opportunity to teach and make public presentations. These opportunities forced me to organize my thoughts and ideas into concise concepts which could be grasped easily by students and conference attendees."

Ames says his greatest satisfaction comes from sharing his knowledge of the human resource field with others; helping subordinate staff develop professionally and acquire and apply knowledge and ideas that he facilitated or nurtured; and receiving feedback from former students, conference and seminar attendees, and organizations with whom he has consulted.

His personal fulfillment hinges primarily on job satisfaction, he says, because:

"I have been blessed in having found a career that provides me with job satisfaction. The job or career is not without its frustrations, but on balance job satisfaction is a big winner. After 26 years, I can honestly say I am excited to come to work, and that I am stimulated and challenged with my job. I continue to learn and to search for new and innovative solutions to problems."

Ames adds that this professional satisfaction makes his personal life more satisfying.

"My personal life is made easier because I do not have the stress from a job or work. This permits me the opportunity to concentrate on my family and personal goals. It also allows me the opportunity to achieve a better balance between my personal and professional life. My family recognizes and supports time away for professional activities because they are cognizant of the intrinsic satisfaction I derive from such ventures."

Beth Green

Beth Green describes herself as a "change manager." Being on the cutting edge, taking risks, and being a mentor are characteristics she believes may have contributed to her nomination as an example of a successful human resource professional. She said:

"I hold one of the few vice president positions in human resources found in higher education and I have designed and applied my terminal degree to complement my career. I am very outspoken and enjoy being knowledgeable about the hottest or newest subjects in our field. I am often invited to take new and difficult assignments.

Another factor in my nomination was probably my colleagues in the professional association who are incredibly supportive mentors. Without their nurturing and support, neither this nomination nor the career growth I have enjoyed would have been possible."

Green identified certain characteristics she says lead to success and separated them into personal and professional traits.

Personal
   * integrity and honesty without brutal frankness;
   * caring, trust, and warmth;
   * a balance of family, friends, recreation, and spirituality;
   * intellect, reliability, energy, and physical fitness; and
   * a sense of humor.

Professional
   * commitment, creativity, and accomplishment;
   * organization, discipline, and decisiveness;
   * direction and a sense of the future;
   * critical knowledge of the human resource field;
   * public relations and problem solving skills;
   * listening skills, intuition, pragmatism, and credibility;
   * tolerance or appetite for change and risk;
   * political savvy; and,
   * endurance.

Beth Green concluded by saying, "each of these qualities must tie together in an application that serves a purpose and satisfies important personal goals. I do not want an epithet that says 'she was a great professional.' "

Conclusion

The practitioners in this chapter have assessed and analyzed the qualities and philosophies they perceive to be responsible for their accomplishments in the human resource management field.

Each profile was interwoven with the lives and careers of other people. Teachers, mentors, superiors, colleagues, family, and the community were mentioned over and over again as playing an important role in their successes. Along with gratitude for those who have helped them along the way, many of those profiled here mentioned that they feel a sense of responsibility to give something back to the community. Most are willing and eager to serve as mentors, volunteers, or role models for others.

The 17 professionals profiled here share many of the characteristics identified in Chapter One. Let's look more closely at the factors common to both the research literature and the human resource professionals profiled.

Proactive Orientation

While the career paths of nominees may have varied considerably depending on education, experience, age, and environment, all of the professionals profiled shared the same proactive attitude.

Proactive phrases were repeatedly used such as "know what you want to achieve." "Be motivated and . . . motivate others." "Develop innovative ways to solve problems."

Proactive words such as "creative," "leadership skills," "risk-taking," "future-oriented," keep appearing over and over in the profiles. Some referred to themselves as a "change manager," "visionary," or as a manager who "empowers others." They view life as a positive experience and welcome challenges that spur their creative energies in a proactive manner. As one respondent said, "I work very hard at anticipating needs rather than reacting to problems."

Communication

Along with a proactive orientation, human resource professionals seem to believe it is important to be skilled communicators. Knowing how to develop programs and solve problems are important, but without the communication skills to persuade others, human resource professionals will not be very effective in their relationships with their supervisors, employees, or peers.

One respondent said, "If you do not have the ability to communicate effectively, your relationships with others will not be fruitful." Of all of the skills related to communication, empathy was cited as one of the most important for it allows professionals to "have the sensitivity and capacity to place yourself in the shoes of another."

Integrity

Almost every one of the human resource professionals profiled here mentioned the importance of having standards, "spiritual grounding," or a code of ethical behavior as part of a successful personal and professional life. As one man stated, "My success, or lack thereof, has been determined, in great measure, by whether or not I am perceived as being totally honest." Others mention words such as "conscientious," "honesty," "trust," "being responsible," and "promoting good standards," as important to their personal and professional well-being.

Flexibility and Adaptability

Innovation, adaptability, and flexibility are viewed as important traits by most human resource managers profiled here. As one person said, "I believe the successful human resource professional must have a high tolerance for ambiguity and a talent for managing multiple and shifting priorities."

One nominee said the adaptability and flexibility necessary to be effective in human resource management actually increased his job satisfaction. He said, "I continue to learn to search for new and innovative solutions to problems. The professional stimulation and satisfaction translates into personal satisfaction."

Technical Proficiency

Also mentioned frequently as important to the human resource professionals is having a critical knowledge of the human resource field and commiting the time and energy to stay current with the literature, policies, and practices. Almost everyone mentioned the importance of being actively involved in professional organizations in the human resource field, writing papers, and public speaking. As one professional put it, "I have always tried to get to know as many fellow professionals as possible to pick their brains for things they are doing well so that I could improve my programs."

A recent publication from the Society for Human Resource Management (SHRM) echoed these same thoughts:

"Are you a technician or business thinker? No longer will technical proficiency in the various human resource functional areas be adequate. Technical proficiency is not just required but expected. The human resource leader of the '90s must command a thorough, in-depth business perspective. The integration of technical proficiency with bottom-line business orientation is the key to transforming the human resource manager and the human resource department from an administrative function focused on functional specialties, to a member of the senior management team, a member whose insights provide a source of competitive advantage for the organization."

In addition to these five traits, several other characteristics frequently noted as essential to effective human resource management were:

* humor,
* giving back to the community,
* developing interests outside of work, and
* family support.

From the foregoing discussion, the senior professionals in this study appear to have many of the same attributes as outlined in the literature as being common to successful management. But in addition to their self-assessments, their performance is evaluated by their CEOs and peers. Let's now turn to the CEOs' comments for a different perspective on the role of effective human resource professionals.

3

CEOs and the Human Resource Professional

The intimacy of the professional relationship between the CEO and the human resource manager was confirmed by CEOs who responded to the invitation to comment on the individuals profiled here. We informally asked the CEOs what characteristics they valued in the successful human resource professional. Their answers shed light on more than just characteristics of successful individuals—they put into focus the role CEOs see the human resource professional playing in the total organization. Viewing "the big picture" from the CEO's vantage point and learning what traits they value in their senior management team sheds light on how good relationships between the HR professional and the CEO have developed.

Note: As with the human resource professionals, the identity of the CEOs will not be included with their comments. They are not identified here so that we might emphasize the content of the CEOs' messages and pinpoint their expectations, rather than identify specific individuals or organizations.

A Fortune 100 CEO

This chief executive is one who retained the chief human resource officer selected by his predecessor. His reasons for continuation were:

1. Business leaders around the country listed him as one of the three best human resource people they had met.
2. The human resource executive knew the company and the new CEO respected him and his work.
3. His wisdom and advice was sound.

The CEO described his relationship with the human resource executive:

"I had known him (earlier) as division head of personnel. I consulted him often and was never disappointed with his wisdom and advice. I was, therefore, delighted when appointed CEO, to have him as my 'Chief of Staff,' head of human resources, and most importantly chief counsel. We met daily then in the office sometimes several times a day.

Together we planned the human side of the remaking of the company, an undertaking that employed well everything he had learned and taught over the years in terms of:

* Employee selection
* Motivation
* Doing the right thing for people in handling staff reductions
* Coaching the CEO
* Moving about the organization putting a hand in here, a word in there, making everything work."

The CEO continued his analysis of what made this match a

"good fit." He described the human resource professional using these adjectives:

1. Selfless (something every human resource person must learn; not all do).
2. Wise.
3. Motivational. (His speech to the company's 100 top managers should be shown to every human resource class.)
4. Practical.
5. Reliable.
6. Innovative.
7. Argues for his point of view with the CEO and wins gracefully or loses but then accepts the decision the CEO has made.
8. Developer of his own department people.

The CEO goes on to say that,

"Probably the most important role of a senior staff person is as the CEO's chief counselor. As such, he or she helps shape the vision, helps communicate it, and encourages others to follow. Their role is not to create the vision—that belongs to the CEO."

This CEO concludes,

"Symbiotic describes an interdependency for mutual gain. In plants and animals it is based on the need for survival. In humans, when practiced at the highest level, it starts with mutual respect and continues because it's fun and productive."

This CEO's assessment of the proper role for an effective and highly valued HR professional matches the five characteristics pointed out earlier. He says he expects: (1) technical proficiency (i.e., he "knew the company," "I was never disappointed with his advice," "CEO's chief counselor"); (2) proactive orientation (i.e., "innovative," "together we planned the human side of the remaking of the company," "moving about the organization putting a hand in here, a word in there"); (3) integrity (i.e., "selfless," "reliable," "doing the right thing for people"); (4) communication skills (i.e., "motivational," "developer of department people"); (5) adaptability and flexibility (i.e., "argues for his point of view with the CEO and wins gracefully or loses, but then adopts the decision").

A Northeastern University President

The president of this mid-sized university focuses on personal qualities when describing the human resource professional at his school.

> "She combines three strengths that I have found most uncommon. First, she has an extraordinary empathy for and understanding of the great richness of possibility inherent in the human condition. Second, she has an intellectual capacity to place any problem or challenge in a larger context, in a longer time frame, and from a variety of perspectives. Third, she has a persuasiveness and drive that achieves results beyond ordinary expectation. The strengths of a dreamer, a planner, and a doer are evidenced rarely in the same individual."

Again, the CEO identifies traits similar to the five we have mentioned.

A Multi-Campus University President

From nearly 20 years of experience in higher education administration, this multi-campus university president gave the following assessment of the successful attributes of his chief human resource executive.

"I consider her to rank among the very best leaders that I have encountered in the field of human resource management. She is extraordinarily knowledgeable of the extensive literature, the state-of-the-art technology, and the latest conceptual developments in the field. Her area is easily the most sensitive one the University has to deal with in terms of excessive regulation by other state agencies, and she has managed those relationships with great tact, sensitivity, and skill. She has demonstrated excellent leadership in the area of affirmative action hiring and retention, an area that is of special significance in this state.

I have had numerous opportunities to work first-hand with her and her staff in all of these dimensions of her work, and I have been consistently impressed by her professionalism and her ability to move the University forward in the field of employee relations."

Again we see the same traits identified by the CEO when discussing his chief human resource executive: "extraordinarily knowledgeable" (technical expertise), "demonstrated excellent leadership" (communication skills), "managed relationships with great tact, sensitivity," "professionalism" (integrity), "her area is easily the most sensitive one the University has to deal with" (adaptability and flexibility), and the "ability to move the university forward" (proactive orientation).

A Professional Organization CEO

Successful professional association executives and human resource professionals have common bonds in that both must understand the nuances of the profession and strive to advance the profession. Consequently, the CEO of a professional organization should possess in-depth knowledge of what it takes to be successful in that field.

One association chief executive described the attributes he looks for in a first rate human resource executive.

* "Mastery of the field of human resource management both in terms of technical knowledge as well as management skills."

* "Administrative capabilities and the ability to apply these skills not only as a science but as an art. One must have the ability to coordinate the disparate parts into a functioning whole with ease and aplomb. In addition, a successful professional in the human resource field must be able to integrate the human and financial resources to ensure productive results."

* "Contemplative—the ability to reflect on issues, problems, situations, and other challenges in a deliberative, reflective way to ensure sound decision making."

* "Adaptive—the ability to confront new situations and ways of operating which are different and adapt well and readily assimilate the new way. Flexibility—taking positions on issues and communicating your position. Being open to other opinions; the ability to accommodate different stands or actions even though they disagree with your position."

* "Fair—listen to all ideas. Treat people and ideas fairly without bias. Deal with matters in an equitable way."

* "Creative—develop ideas that are broad based or ideas that resolve particularly difficult problems."

In addition to the original five traits, this CEO also places great emphasis on the art of "contemplation," which he describes as "the ability to reflect on issues, problems, situations, and other challenges in a deliberative, reflective way to ensure sound decision making."

A Research University President

Administering a research institution with approximately 20,000 employees and 56,000 students requires a CEO and management team that move together like the parts of a fine Swiss watch. The CEO in this study said he looks for qualities such as global thinking, visibility, and accountability. He describes his incumbent human resource officer as a "first rate" person and a "classy professional." He also says:

"He is a dedicated professional who combines a big picture approach with a genuine sensitivity to the University's responsibility to its staff members and their families. He has consistently demonstrated, through the inauguration of special initiatives, a keen awareness of the role of human resource development in the context of a large, public research university. He has shaped a program and recommended policies for the institution that are forward looking, inventive, and effective."

A former CEO of the same institution pinpointed the strengths that she found in this same incumbent's management style.

* "Personnel mattered to him. They were his clients."
* "He accepts hostility and remains calm and listens."
* "He considers alternatives."
* "He looks for new ways to do things; finds new approaches."
* "He analyzes data and uses it productively."

Once again, integrity, communication skills, flexibility and adaptability, proactive orientation, and technical proficiency are the traits the CEO values in the human resource professional.

An Agency CEO

Agencies generally serve extremely important roles as facilitators, regulators, and monitors of the activities of a group of similar entities. These bodies, if managed well, exert great influence. With human resources accounting for a large portion of the organization's total resources, it is no wonder that the effective human resource professional is highly valued by the CEO and plays an integral role in the overall success of the organization. The CEO of one agency supported this premise in evaluating the performance of the chief human resource officer.

"She is a potent force in this organization, partly because of her personality and visibility and also because she has walked a fine line between being the advocate for the staff on a variety of issues and, at the same time, serving as an important part of management. She is constantly walking the halls of this place, feeling the pulse. One of the real differences between her and the others I have known in comparable positions is that she does not allow herself to get bogged down in rigid procedures. While permitting flexibility in the process, she is always zealous in protecting the integrity of the systems over which she presides."

A Religiously Affiliated University CEO

The chief executive officer of this well-known religiously affiliated institution delineated the following characteristics of success in his current human resource executive.

1. She is a very capable student of all of the intricacies associated with the human resource profession.
2. She is personally devoted to the people she is serving.
3. She has learned to balance the delicate interests of the individual person and the institution she is serving.
4. She has earned the full confidence of all of the people who seek her assistance so that they have a feeling of security and peace of mind after consultation with her.

Conclusion

The operational settings of the chief executive officers quoted above differ, yet the expectations and professional characteristics that they mentioned are similar. Each cites an outstanding knowledge of human relations, an ability to effectively fulfill the goals for both management and staff, and adaptability and flexibility to solve problems and put forth new ideas without being rigid as key to success.

4

Internal Clients and the Human Resource Professional

The human resource professional serves many masters in an organization. Clients may be governing boards, professional peers, middle managers, or the rank and file employees. Each constituent comes with a different set of expectations. The way the constituent views the human resource professional is based on value judgments resulting from one interaction or many interactions.

The constituents who participated in this study generally based assessments on situations in which they and the human resource professional were involved. A professional reputation is made on the basis of these personal interactions. Let's examine whether the comments made by this internal community were in sync with the research findings and the CEO perceptions that were identified earlier.

Personal and Professional Integrity

A university trustee cited attributes of friendliness, knowledge, calm demeanor, efficiency, and effectiveness as characteristic of one human resource professional.

The trustee continued, "She is genuinely liked by subordinates and peers; she is respected by the media, government, and the public; and she is trusted by custodians and colleagues alike."

The trustee acknowledged that her assessment would not have been so glowing "if loyalty wasn't one of her attributes."

Another governing board member was also impressed with one of the successful HR professionals because he inspires respect, trust, and loyalty from those who know him.

"His judgment, common sense, and sense of humor are exemplary. In short, he has been a good role model and a good friend for many of us who are engaged in the complicated and challenging field of human resource management."

"Respect," "trust," "loyalty," "common sense," "a good role model"—all are part of a much larger trait—personal and professional integrity. Even though the internal clients have a different relationship with the human resource professional than with the CEO, their expectations are similar.

Respect and admiration were expressed for one profiled professional because: "she was one of the earlier women human resource practitioners in a predominantly male industry. She performed with excellence in a tough factory environment where she was accepted and admired for her performance by workers and management alike."

One professional peer expressed his admiration for his colleague by using the humor he says has sustained the human resource practitioner. He said,

"He sets high standards and expects those to be exceeded. He is tough-minded, but fair. His genuineness as a person combined with a wonderful sense of humor enable him to develop high levels of trust in both his personal and business relationships. He is a mediocre golfer, his golf score being about the same as his bowling score. He doesn't play tennis well nor is he particularly accomplished at squash. But aside from these frailties, he is one of corporate America's most consummate human resource executives."

Flexibility and Adaptability

The ability to respond to change was cited often as a mark of success. Adaptability was viewed as "reflective of the professional's ability to relate to the science of people management." Throughout the literature on leadership and the commentaries by CEOs, trustees, management peers, and subordinates, adaptive problem solving was seen as a useful tool for the human resource professional. In other words, the model human resource professional was expected to provide alternatives and solutions that take into account the current organizational environment and to create qualitative approaches to the future of the organization.

As one peer stated:

"He is creative and is willing to try new approaches and take calculated risks. He is logical and intuitive, is able to simplify complex matters and easily identify decision alternatives. He is sensitive to the need to include others (in planning), but will not hesitate to take action in critical situations."

Proactive Orientation

While solutions and alternatives are constantly sought from the human resource professional, the ability to advise and counsel management appears to be equally important. The capacity to become involved in the larger picture through strategic planning and organizational development has become an essential qualification for today's human resource professional. The result of this proactive orientation is a role on the senior management team of an organization.

In one organizational model found in a public research institution, the chief human resource executive had a pivotal role in seeking new ways to respond to the complex and rapidly changing human and environmental forces. The successful senior executive was concerned with institutional goals and broad institutional issues. Daily management of the human resource function was delegated to the staff he selected, nurtured, and supported.

His staff saw him as a role model who showed through example that "we must be critical thinkers, informed risk-takers, and consummate professionals, if we are to successfully provide a vision, a sense of purpose, and direction to the human resources function," according to one peer.

One higher education emeritus officer spoke of the incumbent human resource executive as "one of the really greats in his field. He implemented one of the most comprehensive and effective bottoms up planning for the total restructuring of personnel service delivery I have ever seen. It was total and effective implementation of participation management."

Good Communication Skills

Personal power of persuasion coupled with the ability to analyze diverse and complex situations can be the force behind moving the human resource function into the mainstream of business planning and business decision making. Examples of successful communication skills were stated clearly and directly by the following comments:

"He has the ability to defuse potentially explosive situations because he can bring adversaries together to resolve their differences. He then shows, with a lot of poise and polish, that the way to resolve a problem is through the process of discussion and give and take."

"Labor and benefit costs, coupled with the continued intrusion of federal, state, and local government into the business decision making process requires that the human resources function be at the center of decision making in a company."

Technical Proficiency

Organizational development and strategic planning are rooted in understanding the organizational culture as a whole. One individual in an executive management position described why he believed the chief human resource officer in his organization had been successful.

"He is broad in his interests and knowledge of the whole organization, including planning, budgeting, the political context within which we operate, and the role and character of the governing board. Without such a broad organizational perspective, the chief human resource officer cannot fully serve the organization."

Another professional colleague said,

"She is recognized by members of the college community as the ultimate resource when assistance is needed on personnel and benefit issues. She has perspective. She is extremely adept at sorting out situations, helping people identify the real issues, and coming up with tactical solutions."

An understanding of the organizational structure, culture, and politics carries even more weight when collective bargaining is involved. The chief human resource executive is part of the collective bargaining team if not the chief negotiator. In addition to in-depth knowledge of the science of human resource management, those involved with collective bargaining must be versed in the National Labor Relations Act and its attendant regulations.

Several of the successful human resource professionals made their reputations in the field of labor relations. One of these individuals was characterized as the "father of labor relations in higher education." The key to his success was described by one of his colleagues.

"The hallmark of his career has been his ability to establish an excellent working and personal relationship with everyone on both sides of what, by design, is an adversarial situation. While doing an excellent job of safeguarding management's interests in every situation, his obvious goal has been to stabilize a good working relationship with all union representatives; the result being enhancing the fulfillment of the mission of the institution."

In another description of a successful human resource executive the writer pointed to leadership positions in professional associations:

"His keen sense of national priorities affecting labor/management relations and national employment policy has enabled him to provide strong leadership in the cutting edge issues. He is a frequent visitor to Washington and on numerous occasions has worked on the front lines or behind the scenes to influence a piece of legislation vital to the business sector."

Proactive Orientation

Creative people have clever ideas, but implementing those ideas is a different proposition which must take into account the overall impact in both the short and long terms. One must also have the ability to persuade others to buy into the concept.

An example of a practitioner who is known for her capacity to see the totality of a situation follows:

> "She sees the big picture in all of our projects. She continually sees new opportunities and has an unusual ability to 'leverage' success through networking people and ideas. Along with her capacity to see the big picture is her ability to take a long-range view. She is able to balance short and long-range needs, recognizing that quality takes time and that progress comes in incremental steps."

An important aspect of taking a long-range view is the ability to predict important trends. Being on the cutting edge of any field requires finely honed skills. Examples of these skills were found in one chief personnel officer who sits on his corporation's Board of Directors.

He was described as follows:

> "He is one of a few personnel professionals to serve on his company's Board. He typifies today's successful HR professional because he has moved the HR function into the mainstream of business planning and business decision making. Personally, his ability to listen, his ability to analyze diverse and complex situations, and his ability to sell his function's point of view to his many clients, are major attributes which have enabled him to attain personal and professional success."

A human resource colleague from a major manufacturing company defines skills that are essential to being effective.

"Effectiveness in the HR field begins at the personal level. One must be thoughtful, deeply concerned about people and social issues, and be an excellent listener. Openness to new ideas from diverse sources is imperative."

Professional Development

In addition to personal qualities, human resource professionalism should be supported by a thorough knowledge of business strategies and practices. The professional needs to maintain his or her technical expertise to contribute to the organization and to the human resource management field by devoting time to public policy leadership and professional associations.

Human resource program planning and development skill provides visibility and an arena for demonstrating leadership. The following examples of leadership exhibited in the area of program development were given by colleagues:

"She is cognizant of the changing role of HR management and what it means to the successful operation of an institution. She provides leadership to her own people as well as the organization-at-large in all matters of training, affirmative action, classification, compensation, and other areas of HR management."

"With salary and wages accounting for three-quarters of the expenditures of many colleges and universities, the effective use of an institution's human resources are recognized to be vital in meeting its mission. She has always believed it to be important to have a human resource management and support system which is sensitive to the many dimensions of the employee rather than focusing on only one or two aspects of the employment relationship. Through the development and maintenance of a comprehensive array of human resource programs and practices, our institution has been able to attract, select, and retain quality employees."

The relationship between representatives of the internal community and the human resource professional differs from the CEO/ HR professional relationship. Consequently, we would not expect the internal colleagues to be quite as concerned with technical proficiency, proactive orientation, or the individual's strategic planning ability as they are concerned with interpersonal relationships, personal and professional integrity, appropriate use of power, and professional development skills.

But, the comments made here by the governing boards, management and professional peers, middle management, and the "rank and file" employees do parallel, to some degree, those identified in previous chapters. Technical proficiency, and proactive orientation are mentioned as important, and internal colleagues also value adaptability and flexibility, communication skills, integrity, and a sense of humor.

Now, let's turn to the comments of the external community.

5

The External Community
and the
Human Resource Professional

A professional reputation results from job performance, perception, word of mouth, leadership roles in community and professional associations, consulting, and even from myth. Whatever the basis for a reputation earned in the human resource profession, interpersonal relationships play a significant role. Educators, consultants, community leaders, and business associates shared their opinions about why an individual is perceived as a professional success.

From educators we heard and read descriptions such as "persuasive," "facilitator," "keen intellect," "teacher," "speaker," "issue-oriented," "sense of humor," "pro-active," "creative," "visible," "defines and shapes," and "flexible." All are characteristics found throughout the discussions in previous chapters.

Representatives from the external community who commented on attributes of the successful human resource professional usually described individuals with whom they had an interpersonal relationship or interaction.

Business School Deans

From the deans of business schools, for example, these comments were made:

"Human resource people generally are not my favorite people. They tend to be inbred, small, and procedural. Those that I admire come at the field from strategic points of view. They come at the job believing that the human resources of the organization are the most important resources. These professionals grapple with organizational issues as the students of organizations."

"One of the HR professionals that I have interacted with extensively was involved in a major reorganization of a Fortune 100 company. He was the right hand to the CEO in developing the reorganization and incentive plan. This HR professional could be a CEO. He has great breadth, a sense of humor, is easy to talk with, no nonsense, and just a great person."

Another dean elicited a very favorable picture of a human resource professional. He said "Few individuals could claim the influence for which she has claimed little credit or recognition." He went on to say:

"Some might even say that she works in mysterious ways. When a need exists, she is quickly able to empower others and to facilitate a resolution that demonstrates shared decision making and ownership. In an institution whose fundamental purpose is the provision of academic programs for students, she is recognized for providing support for the most valuable resource in meeting its mission, its employees."

A third business school dean stated,

"Let me say at the outset that she has been absolutely professional and trustworthy in all our interactions. She is exceptionally well-versed in human resource theory and practice. Her expertise has been recognized by the faculty of our Department of Management. On several occasions she has been invited as a guest lecturer in the areas of compensation administration, corporate recruitment strategies, employee assessment, and other human resource management issues."

The dean stressed other areas of note such as success in shaping the philosophy and direction of the organization's HR programs.

"She is an articulate and persuasive spokesperson for the various constituents who are affected by our personnel policies and procedures. Our policies and programs are progressive and enlightened. They reflect a fundamental respect and concern for our employees."

Academicians

Another group of individuals from the academic arena, the scholars, were liberal in their praise of the nominated professionals. About one of the nominees it was said:

"In addition to his competence and good sense, I always liked working with him because he was not just another bureaucrat. He was an elegantly educated and urbane human being, who had read and traveled widely. He could discuss intelligently just about anything you wanted to talk about from the metaphysical poets to pay ranges. He could, therefore, put the everyday issues in a much broader context than most."

An industrial relations scholar worked with one of the successful HR professionals in an industrial relations institute. The institute was responsible for planning and implementing community service activities. He gave his views on the achievements of one of the nominated HR professionals.

"Our services to management were performed more effectively by this professional than by any of his several predecessors. These services included organizing ability, but more importantly recognition of changing needs and interests and creatively responding, both in form and in content. During my tenure we initiated a publication series directed to the needs of practitioners. The nominee wrote several very useful practitioner-oriented publications which played a very important role in our publication and program activities."

The final academician spoke from the vantage point of one who has had several years of continuous interaction with an HR professional. This academician believes that he would have difficulty cataloging all of the characteristics that make one professional a success but he took the time to discuss seven outstanding attributes:

1. "He has an uncommon ability to get outside of a system, be it an organization or this profession, and observe it objectively, assessing how it 'fits' the context within which it has to produce results and then making the necessary changes so as to bring about effectiveness. In a real sense, he does not merely operate within a system but, rather, defines and shapes the system."

2. "To an exceptional degree, the wisdom and insight he brings to bear on human resource questions and problems is an integration of both experience as an executive and a knowledge of sound psychological principles and processes gained through study."

3. "He possesses an understanding gained through executive experience at the very highest echelons of his industrial organization—of business imperatives and how human resource strategy can be shaped to impact significantly and favorably upon a firm's operating and financial performance."

4. "He possesses an understanding of the relationship between individual performance (at all levels of an organization) and organizational success and how to structure and manage this relationship to the benefit of both the individual and the organization. Implicit in this is his deep belief in the dignity of the individual and compassion for others, but, at the same time, a resolve that organizational objectives are to be met."

5. "He possesses exceptional ability to analyze organizational issues and problems, and unerringly sound judgment in this regard. His clarity of thought, ability to get to the heart of a complex matter, and ability to articulate his reasoning are extraordinary."

6. "He has a finely developed ability to prioritize, to focus effort, and to use time effectively and to transmit these attributes to others within any organizational setting of which he is part."

7. "He is an extremely effective communicator. Both in group deliberations and teaching situations he is highly articulate, persuasive, and even inspiring."

Consultants and Business Associates

In addition to the academicians, the external community category includes consultants and business associates. Their comments indicated respect for the HR professionals and mirrored the characteristics identified by earlier respondents:

"As a leader he is a social architect. He understands organizations and shapes the way they work. His capacity for translating the booming, buzzing confusion of organizational life into meaning is nothing short of amazing. Whether in daily work or in community activities, he elicits the best in any organization with which he is associated."

"She is successful not only because of her dedication, but also because of her depth of knowledge in so many areas. She has gained great respect in the benefits field because she attempts to learn everything she can about issues such as plan design or pending legislation, always analyzing information in relation to the human resource function."

"He was a member of the Hospital Advisory Board; he chaired the Human Resource Committee. In that role, he provided direction for our overall HR plan including development and oversight of the recruitment and retention programs for staffing an additional 200 beds; assistance and direction with development of the Affirmative Action plan; the revamping of the entire Wage and Salary Program, including a Performance Evaluation Program; and development of a Career Ladder Program. In each of these areas, he not only sets the direction and tone, but also has the ability to call forth the best from other committee members, as well as to properly challenge and motivate the staff."

"She has evidenced conceptual skills, dealing with a variety of complex human resource issues. But more importantly, she has combined a high degree of innovation and managerial excellence in the development of human resource programs with outstanding interpersonal skills. It is unusual to have the two qualities combined so successfully—regardless of the organization's size."

Conclusion

This informal analysis of characteristics exhibited by successful human resource practitioners sheds some light on what it takes to succeed in the profession.

From the perspective of the CEOs interviewed, strategic planning and the ability to make sound decisions after contemplating the options are the most valued assets of their human resource officers. From the human resource professionals and their internal colleagues' perspectives, communication skills, empathy, trust, and even humor are valued assets. Academicians stress education, articulation, and intellectual capabilities.

Some of these characteristics can be taught, others result from life experiences, and still others are rooted in individual personality traits. Whatever the source for obtaining these essential qualities and characteristics, the 17 individuals we have profiled here not only exemplify these traits but believe them to be the basis of their success in the human resource profession.

6

*Profiles
of
Success*

The following 17 human resource professionals represent a sample of the many outstanding practitioners in the field who, through their continuous contributions to the profession, move the human resource function and profession from the periphery to the center of management.

Robert L. Berra, SPHR

Robert L. Berra, SPHR, began his human resource career in 1947 on the faculty of the School of Business at St. Louis University. He then began a career with the Monsanto Company that spanned three decades including two decades as vice president for personnel in the company's St. Louis headquarters.

Berra holds an MBA from Harvard University and has authored many articles in the area of management and motivation. He has served as a guest lecturer at numerous universities including Harvard Graduate School of Business, Washington University, St. Louis University, University of South Carolina, University of Nebraska, and University of Michigan.

He is past president of the Industrial Relations Association of Greater St. Louis and a past-president and a member of the Executive Committee of the Society for Human Resource Management (formerly the American Society for Personnel Administration). He is a 1977 recipient of the Alumni Merit Award from St. Louis University and the recipient of the ASPA Professional of the Year Award in 1983.

Berra serves on several community boards of trustees and is an adjunct faculty member at two universities. Prior to his retirement, he was a member of the Board of Directors of Monsanto Company, Fisher Controls International, Inc., G.D. Searle & Company, and the NutraSweet Company.

Ronald A. Bouchard

Ronald A. Bouchard's 27-year human resource career has included various positions in institutions of higher education. He currently serves as associate vice president for personnel administration at the University of Virginia.

Bouchard has held leadership positions in every professional association and community organization with which he has been affiliated. He served as president of the College and University Personnel Association in 1980-81 and has held many other offices within the association. He is the author of *Personnel Practices for Small Colleges*, co-published by CUPA and the National Association of College and University Business Officers, and is a co-author of the *Interview Guide for Supervisors*, which is currently in its third edition. He has conducted more than 50 professional development programs and has published numerous articles in the scholarly journals of CUPA, NACUBO, and *Independent School Management*.

Bouchard is a human resource consultant to institutions of higher education. He has received awards from the Indiana Jaycees, the Outstanding Young Man of America Award, and the College and University Personnel Association's Donald E. Dickason Award—the highest award given by the association for continued distinguished service to the profession. He has also been the recipient of CUPA's Kathryn G. Hansen Publications Award.

Bouchard holds an MA in management from Ball State University.

Barbara Butterfield

Dr. Barbara Butterfield is the vice president for human resources at Stanford University. Throughout her 25-year career as a higher education administrator she has developed a proven track record in planning, systems, people, and risk management. She has developed a long-range analysis and strategy in workforce demographics, management and cost containment for the University of Pennsylvania; implemented an extremely successful bargained contract while maintaining the respect of the union members at Duke University; served Michigan State University as director of personnel administration; and served for 17 years at Southern Illinois University at Carbondale, culminating in the top HR management position.

She has published numerous articles in the *CUPA Journal* on topics such as effective merit pay, management by objectives, and planned employment of the culturally and economically disadvantaged. Her *Planned Programed Management,* a management by objectives, accountability, budget, and human resource development concept for Southern Illinois University was published in 1972.

Dr. Butterfield serves on the College and University Personnel Association's Publications and Research Advisory Board. She holds M.S. and Ph.D. degrees in education administration from Southern Illinois University, and is a graduate of the Advanced Management Institute of the Wharton School of Business.

Bruce Carswell

Bruce Carswell is senior vice president of human resources and administration and director, GTE Corp. Elected to the position in March, 1986, he provides counsel and support to both the GTE chairman and the president. He began his 33-year career with GTE Sylvania in 1958 as staff attorney and was named a division and staff counsel for labor relations in 1961, vice president of industrial relations in 1970, vice president of human resources in 1976, and senior vice president of human resources and administration for GTE Corp. in 1986.

In his current position, Carswell directs the activities of the human resources, internal communications, and headquarters administration departments and is a member of the Policy Committee of GTE, a multinational corporation operating in 46 states and 41 countries, with combined revenues and sales of $16.5 billion and net income of $1.2 billion (in 1988).

In addition, Carswell is a member of the New York State Bar Association and the labor section of the American Bar Association. He is a member of the executive committee and past chairman of the Employee Relations Committee of the Business Roundtable and is chairman of the Board of Directors of the Labor Policy Association. He also serves on the board of directors of various other professional and volunteer organizations and is a past member of the Board of Directors of St. Joseph's Hospital in Stamford and a past Vice President and member of the Board of Governors of the White Plains, N.Y., Hospital Association. He received his bachelor's degree from Colby College, and his LLB from Cornell University.

Joyce A. Fecske

Joyce Fecske is vice president for human resources at DePaul University, where she has spent most of her 21-year career in human resource management. Previously, Fecske was DePaul's executive assistant to the president and director of personnel. She has been chairperson of the College and University Personnel Association's Council on Fringe Benefits and has served on similar committees for the National Association of College and University Business Officers and the National Association of Independent Colleges and Universities.

Fecske has presented programs on tax and benefits issues over the last decade relating to health care cost management, retirement counseling, complying with pension and welfare nondiscrimination rules, microcomputer applications for benefit programs, employee assistance programs, and flexible benefits. Recognized as an expert on employee fringe benefits design, Fecske assisted in the planning and production of CUPA's first videotape, "Ready, Set, Go"— a primer on retirement planning, and participated in the first national teleconference produced by the American Council on Education on "Early Retirement Incentives and Career Change Options."

Fecske holds BA and MA degrees in philosophy from DePaul University.

Suzanne M. Forsyth, AEP

Suzanne M. Forsyth has 25 years of executive management experience in associations, education, and business environments. She currently serves as the director of human resources for the American Council on Education where she created and directs an integrated human resource department.

Forsyth has served in leadership positions with organizations such as the Society for Human Resource Management, the United Way, the National Faculty Exchange, and Women Administrators in Higher Education.

She has served as the Executive Secretary of the Washington Higher Education Secretariate, a consortium of higher education associations in Washington, D.C., since 1973.

She has been a speaker before many organizations including the American Council on Education, the National Council on the Aging, the College and University Personnel Association, the International Personnel Management Association, and the American Management Association, on human resource-related topics ranging from changing demographics and workforce diversity to performance appraisal and other personnel practices.

Forsyth has served as a human resource management consultant for education, business, and government. For her contributions to the stature of the human resource profession within higher education, she was awarded the Diedrich K. Willers Award of the College and University Personnel Association's Eastern Region.

Ray T. Fortunato

Ray T. Fortunato is president of Ray T. Fortunato Associates, a consulting firm experienced in higher education administration with an emphasis on the human resource field covering the administration of faculty and staff personnel affairs. He retired from Pennsylvania State University as assistant vice president for personnel administration where he was responsible for personnel programs for 22 campuses including a medical center. He has been in higher education personnel administration for over 30 years.

Fortunato is past-president of the College and University Personnel Association and received its highest honor, the Donald E. Dickason Award, in 1972, and the Eastern Region's Diedrich K. Willers Award in 1979. He has served as chairman of the Eastern Universities Personnel Group and president of the Centre County Personnel Association. In 1986, he was awarded Penn State's John E. Wilkinson Award for administrative excellence and in 1987, Penn State's Lion's Paw Medal.

He has co-authored several books on personnel administration in higher education including: *Personnel Administration in Higher Education (A Handbook on Faculty and Staff Personnel Practices in Colleges and Universities)*, published by Jossey-Bass, Inc.; *Handbook for Developing Higher Education Personnel Policies, Human Resource Development in Higher Education,* and *Higher Education Personnel Forms,* published by the College and University Personnel Association; and coordinated the publication of a collection of essays entitled *Essential Personnel Practices.* His publications for CUPA have earned him the distinction of being the only four-time recipient of the Kathryn G. Hansen Publications Award (in 1982, 1983, 1986, and 1988).

He has served on the faculty of NACUBO's College Business Management Institute at the University of Kentucky; has spoken at meetings of the National Association of College and University Business Officers, the American Council on Education and the College and University Personnel Association; and has served as a consultant to more than 50 institutions of higher education on faculty and staff personnel issues.

R. Kenneth Hutchinson

R. Kenneth Hutchinson is associate vice president, human resource services for the University of Missouri System. Hutchinson has served either the Missouri System or its branch campuses in a human resource function over the past 25 years. In his current position, he serves as the chief human resource officer for 13,900 employees at four campuses with a total enrollment of 56,000 students. In this corporate capacity, he has responsibility for policy development and administration in the areas of labor/employee relations, compensation, faculty and staff benefits, recruitment, professional development, affirmative action, and personnel information systems. He serves as the chief spokesperson for the university during labor negotiations for the four campuses and the hospital and clinic.

Hutchinson represented the University of Missouri on the statewide Council of Missouri State College and University

Business Officers from 1984-89, has been a faculty member for the Association of Physical Plant Administrators' Institute for Facilities Management; served as a member of the Board of Directors of the Personnel Research Forum of Greater Kansas City; and president of the Personnel Management Association of Columbia, MO.

He was president of the College and University Personnel Association during 1989-90 and chair of CUPA's Midwest Region in 1982. In 1991 he was the recipient of the Donald E. Dickason Award, CUPA's highest award for distinguished service.

Hutchinson holds a master's degree in higher education administration from the University of Missouri-Columbia.

Jane Jameson

Jane Jameson is senior vice president for personnel at the University of South Carolina where she has served nearly 20 years in various human resource-related positions in classification, compensation, personnel services, and affirmative action. As senior vice president, she serves as a member of the senior administrative staff of the university and is responsible for HRM policies and programs for faculty and staff of the nine-campus University of South Carolina System.

Jameson is on the Board of Directors of Pro-Net and the Columbia Personnel Association and has been a member of the College and University Personnel Association's Board of Directors, serving as its Vice President for Membership (1985-87), Southern Region Chair (1984), and on the National Conference Planning Committee (1990). In 1986 she received the Outstanding Achievement Award from CUPA's Southern Region.

She is highly regarded in her community where she is a charter member of the South Carolina Division of Human Resource Management Advisory Committee and serves on the state's Employee Suggestion Review Committee and Information Technology Advisory Board. Her civic involvement includes leadership positions in the Columbia Chamber of Commerce, Rotary Club, Junior League, United Way, and Red Cross. Her volunteer activities over the years have included stints as a hospital emergency room volunteer and as a trainer and listener for a crisis intervention hotline.

Jameson holds a master's degree in public administration from the University of South Carolina.

Caesar J. Naples, J.D.

Caesar J. Naples is vice chancellor for faculty and staff relations at California State University where he is responsible for a systemwide personnel and employee relations program for academic and support staff. Since 1983, Naples has served on the Chancellor's executive staff and as staff to the Board of Trustees of California State University on one or more of its standing committees.

Previous positions held by Naples have included general counsel of the Florida Board of Regents (1976-83) where he was responsible for the development and implementation of a comprehensive employee relations, faculty liaison, personnel, and collective bargaining program for the State University System of Florida; and assistant vice chancellor for employee relations at SUNY-Albany (1971-76) where he served as the chief employee relations officer for all 30 SUNY campuses.

Naples has been a frequent speaker on public sector collective bargaining to organizations such as the National Center for the Study of Collective Bargaining in Higher Education, Baruch College, American Political Science Association, and the American Arbitration Association.

His writings on collective bargaining have been published extensively in scholarly journals and he is the author of chapters on faculty collective bargaining in numerous books published by Jossey-Bass, Inc., and in *Collective Bargaining: The State of the*

Art, published by the College and University Personnel Association.

Dr. Naples holds memberships in the American Bar Association, the Federal Bar Association, the National Association of College and University Attorneys, American Arbitration Association, the College and University Personnel Association, and the American Judicature Society. He serves on the Board of Directors of the National Center for the Study of Collective Bargaining in Higher Education and is co-founder of the Academy of Academic Personnel Administration, the national organization of university chief labor relations officers.

He received his BA from Yale and his J.D. from SUNY-Buffalo.

Ann K. Otto

Ann K. Otto is assistant vice provost for administration and director of human resources for Northeastern Ohio Universities College of Medicine where she developed a comprehensive human resource program responsible for employment, EEO, training and development, compensation, institutional health and safety, employee relations, benefits, and policies and procedures relating to human resources and organization development issues. Her career has included human resource-related positions in higher education, business, and industry.

Her professional and community affiliations have included president of the Portage Chapter of the American Society for Personnel Administration; member of the College and University Personnel Association's Publications and Research Advisory Board (1981-86); Program Chair, Ohio Chapter, American Society for Training and Development; Ohio Association of Women Deans, Administrators and Counselors; Portage County Mortar Board Alumni, President; Tallmadge Middle School PTA Board; and Portage County Safety Council.

She has published articles on issues relating to unfair labor practices of employee unions, and served as editor of a special wage and salary issue of the *CUPA Journal*.

Otto holds a master's degree in education from Kent State University where she is currently working on her Ph.D.

Katie Smothers

Katie Smothers is human resource and business manager at the University of California-San Diego where she oversees the administration of a $34 million facilities management budget, a $42 million employment and training grant including Federal Reporting and Contracts Management, and a general services information systems budget of $18 million.

She is an expert on organizational development and planning and has served as a liaison between the public and private sector through "blue ribbon" panels, ad hoc teams, and task forces on personnel management issues.

Smothers is a member of the Association of Physical Plant Administrators (APPA) and has served as a faculty member for the APPA Institute for Facilities Management. She is an Executive Board Member and Trustee of the La Jolla Town Council, and serves on the Board of Directors of the San Diego International Visitors Council and the Citizens' Advisory Group of the San Diego Police Department (Northern Division).

John A. Spitz

John A. Spitz is director of the State of Washington's Higher Education Personnel Board where he is responsible for developing and implementing human resource practices for 16,000 non-faculty employees in Washington State's public colleges and universities. Successful programs that were developed under his direction include a comprehensive classification and compensation system for 1,000 state employees; development of a family leave program and a program to provide reasonable accommodation for disabled employees; the development of an intricate pay equity system, and a computerized applicant tracking system for affirmative action.

As the director of the state's Higher Education Personnel Board, Spitz also serves as a consultant to 33 campus personnel officers who administer the state system. Spitz is a member of the State of Washington Productivity Board and an ex officio member of the Governors' Affirmative Action Policy Committee. He previously served as Chairman of the Center for Management, Research and Education at the Institute of Industrial Relations at UCLA. While there, he developed quality educational materials and training programs for human resource managers and contributed to a number of publications on public sector labor relations and other topics in human resource management.

He holds an MBA in industrial relations from DePaul University.

James R. Thiry

James R. Thiry is assistant vice president for personnel at the University of Michigan where he plans and coordinates the university personnel programs, policies, and procedures for all professional and administrative staff, including more than 16,000 non-instructional staff members.

Other than a brief period in the early '70s, Thiry has been with the University of Michigan since 1964 in various human resource-related positions including director of personnel, manager of staff and union relations, and assistant manager, staff benefits.

He has been a member of the College and University Personnel Association for more than 27 years and is CUPA's president-elect for the 1991-92 academic year. He has also served as CUPA's Vice President for Membership Services (1988-90); Chair of the National Conference Program (1988); Past National Chair of the Council on Labor Relations; Past Chair of the Upstate New York

Chapter; and chair of the Midwestern Region.

Thiry is also affiliated with the Association of Physical Plant Administrators and serves as a faculty member of APPA's Institute for Facilities Management.

Martha A. Turnbull

Martha Turnbull has been director of personnel services at Ithaca College since 1976. She is responsible for the formulation, interpretation, and administration of personnel policies and practices including employee relations, benefits, wage and salary administration, recruitment and selection, records, and training and development for over 1,100 employees of the private four-year college. Her human resource career has included work for the A.C. Nielsen Company and the Littlewoods Organization in Oxford, England where she was responsible for all aspects of the human resource function in a large retail organization.

In addition to having served as chair of the Eastern Region of the College and University Personnel Association, Turnbull is affiliated with the Society for Human Resource Management, the Ithaca Personnel Association, and the Ithaca Management Council.

She holds a master of arts degree from Cornell University and a Management Certificate from Oxford Polytechnic's Institute of Personnel, Oxford, England. She has also taught undergraduate courses in compensation administration and personnel management at Ithaca College and Tompkins Cortland Community College.

William F. Waechter

Dr. William F. Waechter is vice chancellor, human resources, of the Maricopa Community College District in Phoenix, Arizona. His professional career in higher education has spanned three decades beginning in 1963 as professor of sociology and political science at Long Beach Community College District. He became dean of instruction at that school in 1969 and served as director of personnel services from 1971-79. From 1979 to 1984, he served in various capacities at Coast Community College District and Webster University.

Dr. Waechter has written articles and presented papers on a wide variety of topics in human resource management including wellness in the workplace, HR practices for community colleges, classification of employees, and affirmative action. He has served as a consultant to the American Council on Education's Equal Pay in Higher Education Task Force; Santa Monica City College Administrators Association; the Association of California Community College Administrators; and the School Employers Association.

He holds membership in the College and University Personnel Association, the American Management Association, the Society for Human Resource Management, the American Arbitration Association, the Arizona Industrial Relations Association, and is an associate member of the labor and employment law section of the State Bar of California. In addition, he has served on the Board of Directors of the Long Beach Retarded Children's Foundation, the Rotary Club of Lakewood, and is a charter member of the Association of California Community College Administrators.

He holds an MA from California State University-Long Beach and an Ed.D. in higher education administration from the University of Southern California.

Beth Chandler Warren

Beth C. Warren is associate vice president for human resources, and executive director of the Human Resource Consortium, at the University of Southern Maine. She also currently serves as a part-time associate professor in the University's College of Education, Department of Human Resource Development.

She is involved extensively on community boards of directors and in professional organizations. She is a member of the American Association of University Women, chair of the Maine Human Rights Commission (appointed by Governor John McKernan), chair-elect of the Eastern Region of the College and University Personnel Association, a member of the NAACP of Greater Portland, the National Association of Social Workers, and numerous other non-profit organizations such as Big Brother/Big Sister, YWCA, and the Southern Maine Handicapped Association.

Warren has coordinated and/or presented seminars on such work and family issues as child care, workplace stress, and women in management. Under her direction, the University of Southern Maine has received nearly 50 awards and recognitions since 1984 from the College and University Personnel Association, the Southern Maine Association for the Education of Young Children, the National Association of College and University Business Officers, and the National Association for the Education of Young Children.

She received CUPA's national Creativity Award for the Child Care Renaissance Program at the University of Southern Maine (1987); the Eastern Region's Excellence in Human Resource Management Award for creativity and innovative approaches to human resource management (1990); and the Diedrich K. Willers Award for her outstanding contribution to the human resource profession (1988).

In 1988, she was the recipient of the "Best on the Block" award presented by the Congressional Caucus for Women's Issues in Washington, D.C.

Contributors

The following professionals have contributed their time, their energy, and their comments on their peers for attribution in this monograph.

Donna M. Allen
Dean of Administrative Services,
Olympic College

Samuel G. Andrews
Vice President for Administration
University of Southern Maine

Robert H. Atwell
President
American Council on Education

T.F. Bean (Retired)
Employee Relations Division
Allis Chalmers Corporation

George C. Bedell
Director
University Presses of Florida

A. Lee Belcher (retired)
Vice President
University of Missouri

Forest C. Benedict
Director, Human Resource Services and Analysis
University of Missouri System

Freda Bernatovicz
Research Associate
University of Southern Maine

James F. Brinkerhoff
Vice President Emeritus
University of Michigan

W. Perry Brown
Vice President, Director Personnel Division
American Cyanamid Company

Susy S. Chan
Vice President for University Planning and Research
DePaul University

Mary I. Collins
Staff Development Director
University of Southern Maine

Richard C. Creal
Executive Director
College and University Personnel Association

Madeleine d'Ambrosio
Vice President, Institutional Counseling
Teachers Insurance and Annuity Association
College Retirement Equities Fund

David R. Day
Head, Management Education Programs
University of Illinois at Urbana-Champaign

Frank P. Doyle
Senior Vice President
General Electric Corp.

James M. Elliott
Director of Human Resources
Pennsylvania State University

John T. Farrell
President
St. John's Mercy Medical Center

Robert L. Gale
President
Association of Governing Boards of Universities and Colleges

John N. Gardner
Vice Chancellor, Director, University Professor
  of Library and Information Science
University of South Carolina

Lily Roland Hall
Board of Trustees
University of South Carolina

Anita D. Herington
Secretary to the Board of Trustees
  and the University
Kent State University

Steven J. Ickes
Operations and Staffing
Fairview Training Center

Howard V. Knicely
Executive Vice President
Human Resources, Communications
  and Information Resources
TRW, Inc.

Eleanor W. Law
Special Assistant to the
  Associate Vice President
University of Southern Maine

Thomas D. Layzell
Chancellor
Board of Governors of State Colleges
  and Universities

Robert E. Lefton
Consultant
Psychological Associates

David K. Long
Dean, School of Business,
Ithaca College

George R. Lovette
Vice President Emeritus for
 Business and Operations
Pennsylvania State University

C. Peter Magrath
President
University of Missouri System

Richard J. Mahoney
Chairman and Chief Executive Officer
Monsanto Company

Frank B. Manley
President
Frank B. Manley & Company

Frederic Meyers
 Professor Emeritus of Industrial Relations
University of California at Los Angeles

James T. McGill
Vice President for Administrative Affairs
University of Missouri System

Dorothy D. Moore
Dean, College of Education
University of Southern Maine

Eva Myking
Assistant Director
University of California, San Diego

Allan W. Ostar
President Emeritus
American Association of State
  Colleges and Universities

Rev. John T. Richardson, C.M.
President
DePaul University

Robert C. Richardson
Chair, Higher Education Personnel Board
  Tacoma, Washington

Linda B. Rosenthal
Governing Board Member
Maricopa Community Colleges

Patricia Rueckel
Executive Director
National Association for Women Deans,
  Administrators, and Counselors

Jacob M. Samit
Assistant Vice Chancellor, Employee Relations
California State University

John Scherba
Senior Vice President, Employee Relations
First National Bank of Ohio

Robert F. Schmidt
Director of Personnel Services
Medical College of Wisconsin

Kenneth L. Schwab
Executive Vice President, Administration
University of South Carolina

Carl Sgrecci
Vice President and Treasurer
Ithaca College

Arthur K. Smith
Interim President
University of South Carolina

Barbara S. Uehling
Chancellor
University of California-Santa Barbara

Robert L. Virgil
Dean, John M. Olin School of Business
Washington University in St. Louis

James M. Wagner
Vice President for Business and Operations
Pennsylvania State University

Donald W. Ward
Assistant Vice President for
  Administration and Personnel
University of Illinois

Norman E. Watson
Chancellor Emeritus
Coast Community College District

James J. Whalen
President
Ithaca College

Farris W. Womack
Vice President and Chief Financial Officer
University of Michigan

Robert L. Woodbury
Chancellor
University of Maine System

Bibliography

Andrews, I. R. "Leadership and Supervision." *Encyclopedia of Psychology* 2. New York: John Wiley & Sons, 1984.

Atwater, L. E. "The Relative Importance of Situational and Individual Variables in Predicting Leader Behavior." *Group and Organizational Studies* (1987) 13(3): 290-310.

Batlis, N. C. and Green, P. C. "Leadership Style Emphasis and Related Personality Attributes." *Psychological Reports* 44, (1979): 587-592.

Brecht-Dunbar, T. "Diverse Workforce Will End Discrimination," *HR News,* Society for Human Resource Management (March, 1990).

Destanick, R. "What Makes the Human Resource Function Successful?" *Training and Development Journal* (February, 1984): 41-46.

Fitz-enz, J. "Human Resource Measurement: Formulas for Success." *Personnel Journal* (October, 1985): 53-60.

Gattiker, U. E. and Larwood, L. "Career Success, Mobility and Extrinsic Satisfaction for Corporate Managers," *The Social Science Journal* (1989): 26 (1): 75 92.

Gattiker, U. E. and Larwood, L. "Predictors for Managers' Career Mobility, Success and Satisfaction." *Human Relations* (1988): 1 (8): 569-591.

Korman, A. K., Wittig-Berman, U. and Lang, D. "Career Success and Personal Failure: Alienation in Professionals and Managers," *Academy of Management Journal* (1981): 24: 342-360.

Offermann, L. R. "Visibility and Evaluation of Female and Male Leaders." *Sex Roles* (1986) 14 (9/10): 533-543.

Romero, G. J. and Garza, R. T. "Attributions for the Occupational Success/Failure of Ethnic Minority and Nonminority Women." *Sex Roles* (1986): 14 (7/8).

Solomon, J. "People Power," *The Wall Street Journal* (March, 1990): 33.

Steinberg, J. A. *Climbing the Ladder of Success in High Heels.* Ann Arbor, Michigan: UMI Research Press, 1984.

Wilkins, S. W. and McCullers, J. C. "Personal Factors Related to Typicalness of Career and Success in Active Professional Women. *Psychology of Women Quarterly* (1978): 343-357.

Yoder, D. and Heneman, Jr., H. *ASPA Handbook of Personnel and Industrial Relations.* Bureau of National Affairs, Inc.: Washington, D.C., 1979.